PRAISE FOR
Columns by Nathan W. Tucker
www.nathanwtucker.com

"I think it is very, very good." --Steve Deace [WHO Radio}

"Your command of the material is impressive." --Akron Beacon Journal

"Some excellent posts…!" --Lyle Denniston [SCOTUSBLOG.com]

"Your writing is smart and interesting…" -The Philadelphia Inquirer

"I must credit your originality…Expectedly, I disagree with you but I cannot fault your logic." --Billy Oyadare [Assistant Iowa Public Defender]

WE THE PEOPLE:

THE ONLY CURE TO JUDICIAL ACTIVISM

NATHAN W. TUCKER

InArena Publishing House
www.inarena.com

InArena Publishing House
www.inarena.com

ISBN 978-0-615-36145-1

Printed in the United States of America.

Dedicated to an independent judiciary governed by the sovereign will of the people.

If you would like to learn more about efforts to check judicial activism or to volunteer, please visit Federalist 78 PAC online at www.federalist78.org.

CONTENTS

GIVE US OUR VOTE
April 6, 2009

ON APRIL 3rd, THE IOWA Supreme Court unanimously ruled that Iowa's Defense of Marriage Act (DOMA) was unconstitutional. The court held that the statute. which had limited marriage to a union between one man and one woman, violated the equal protection clause of the Iowa Constitution. Unless the court reverses itself, which seems extremely unlikely, homosexual couples will be able to marry on April 24, 2009.

When we first lobbied the Iowa legislature several years ago on the need to pass a constitutional amendment protecting marriage, the leadership of the Republican Party, the majority party at the time, told us that Iowa's DOMA statute was good enough and that Iowa's judiciary would never overturn it. We pointed out that recent history (Hawaii, Massachusetts, Connecticut, and California) reveals that a state only adopts homosexual

1

marriage by judicial decree. We argued that it is only when the people of a state have a direct vote on the issue is marriage protected.

But the Republican leadership ignored the historical record and now years later, homosexual marriage is a reality in Iowa. Now the Democrats, who control both chambers in the Iowa legislature, show no interest in passing a constitutional amendment protecting marriage. Nor will they, for the issue would tear their party apart between their liberal base and the moderates as they argue over whether to allow full-fledged homosexual marriage, civil unions, domestic partnerships, or nothing at all. The liberal leadership in the party got what they wanted—homosexual marriage— without any cost to party unity and therefore they aren't going to risk open rupture in their party by bringing the issue up for a debate.

And any attempt to pass a constitutional amendment would be met by the argument that proponents of such an amendment are intolerant of two gay people who love each other and simply want the same rights as everybody else. But the argument is misleading because it frames the issue solely as a pro- or anti-gay marriage argument.

The larger issue, however, is not whether homosexuals can marry, but now that gays can marry why can't other unions—such as the bigamous, polygamous, or incestuous—be legal? Nor is this as implausible as it sounds, for the Iowa Supreme Court held that marriage restrictions must be justified by "exceedingly persuasive justification(s)." If marriage is no longer limited to one man and one woman, what justification is there to limit it to a two-person union, or to a union between unrelated people when contraceptives are used?

The court has opened the door to marriage just a little, and it is only a matter of time before it opens it wider yet to allow other unions the same status of marriage as heterosexual couples. But we should learn from the mistakes of the Republican leadership and not wait until such a scenario becomes reality in Iowa. The time to act is now, and to wait is a failure of responsibility. Every state that has voted on the issue, even liberal California, has passed a constitutional amendment protecting marriage, and poll after poll of Iowans reveal that, if allowed, we would join their ranks.

And nothing would be more democratic than a direct vote on the issue by the people themselves. If we are going to redefine an institution as fundamental as marriage, it should be up to the people if, and how, it should be done. And if the majority in the Iowa legislature denies us our vote, we need to vote in new members who will. And if our fundamental right to vote is still denied, we should demand the ability to pass laws and constitutional amendments at the ballot box. The democratic process is broken when the will of the people is frustrated by the politicians in the legislature.

This isn't just a referendum on marriage, but on whether or not the people will be allowed to govern themselves.

Originally published in *The Des Moines Register* on April 23, 2009

Nathan W. Tucker

ENTER THE MATRIX—A CONSTITUTIONAL RIGHT TO SELF-IDENTITY
June 7, 2009

ON APRIL 3, 2009, THE IOWA Supreme Court ruled that Iowa's Defense of Marriage Act (DOMA), which limited marriage to that between one man and one woman, was unconstitutional because it violated the Equal Protection Clause of the State's Constitution. The court's ruling has been touted as a victory for gay marriage, but a fuller reading of the opinion reveals that its implications are far more reaching than just that particular issue.

The "right" found by the Iowa Supreme Court is not, contrary to public opinion, the right to marry. Yes, the court did find a "right to sexual orientation," a nebulous concept the court never bothered to define or limit in any way in its sixty-nine page opinion. But sexual orientation, if it means anything, means one's preference in sexual relations, a definition not limited simply to heterosexual or homosexual relationships but must also include bigamous, polygamous, incestuous, pedophilic, beastious, necrophilia.

The court held that Iowa's DOMA was unconstitutional because homosexuals "cannot simultaneously fulfill their deeply felt need for a committed personal relationship, as influenced by their sexual orientation, and gain the civil status and attendant benefits granted by the [marriage] statute." Marriage as defined by the court, therefore, is simply a "committed personal relationship...influenced by...sexual orientation" that, noticeably, is not limited in any way, even to a monogamous relationship.

But the court did more than declare a constitutional right to sexual orientation that must be entitled to all the marriage benefits that heterosexual couples enjoy. Rather, the court determined that everyone has a right to self-identity. For in finding the right to sexual orientation, it determined that it is not necessary for sexual orientation to be an immutable characteristic.

As the court rightly pointed out, a human trait that defines a group is "immutable" when the trait exists "solely by the accident of birth" or when the person with the trait has no ability to change it. The concept of immutability is important when examining an equal protection claim because the "inability of a person to change a characteristic that is used to justify different treatment makes the discrimination violative of the rather basic concept of our system that legal burdens should bear some relationship to individual responsibility."

Knowing that science has not shown sexual orientation to be immutable, the court redefined immutability to mean that "the identifying trait is so central to a person's identity that it would be abhorrent for government to penalize a person for refusing to change it." Quoting the California Supreme Court, the Iowa Supreme Court held that "[b]ecause a person's sexual orientation is so integral an aspect of one's identity, it is not appropriate to require a person to repudiate or change his or her sexual orientation in order to avoid discriminatory treatment."

"Because sexual orientation is central to personal identity and may be altered, if at all, only at the expense of significant damage to the individual's sense of self," the court held that sexual orientation is now a suspect class "entitled to [the same] consideration as…any other group that has been deemed to exhibit an immutable characteristic."

This concept of personal identity and sense of self is the new "right" found in the Iowa Constitution by judicial fiat. Unfortunately, this right is neither new nor limited to sexual orientation or marriage but has also been used by courts to justify abortion and a right to die. It is the vogue (and vague) right used by courts when they want to read into the constitution rights that aren't there.

The elasticity of this new right can be found in the U.S. Supreme Court's rather utopian explanation of it in its decision in *Planned Parenthood v. Casey* in which it affirmed *Roe v. Wade*:

Our law affords constitutional protection to personal decisions relating to marriage, procreation, contraception, family relationships, child rearing, and education…These matters, involving the most intimate and personal choices a person may make in a lifetime, choices central to personal dignity and autonomy, are central to the liberty protected by the Fourteenth Amendment.

At the heart of liberty is the right to define one's own concept of existence, of meaning, of the universe, and of the mystery of human life. Beliefs about these matters could not define the attributes of personhood were they formed under compulsion of the State. (emphasis added)

Given such an expansive individual right to self identity, government is only possible if its citizens unanimously and freely acquiesced their right to self identity when each new law is passed (a phenomenon not yet experienced in the history of mankind) or by its selective enforcement by the judiciary when it suits their purposes. By picking and choosing which values constitute this right to self identity, our courts have taken it upon themselves cart blanche authority to define for us what our identity really is. This is the Matrix come to life, but with robed judges rather than machines defining our reality.

A MATTER OF CIVIL RIGHTS?
May 8, 2009

IT HAS BECOME A COMMON refrain among proponents of same-sex marriage that it is a matter of civil rights. They argue that fairness and equal protection require that a loving gay couple to be entitled to the same rights as heterosexual couples. The Des Moines Register today reported on a meeting of black leaders yesterday who compared the gay marriage movement to the civil rights movement.

Among those present was Alexander Robinson, the executive director of the National Black Justice Coalition based in Washington, D.C. which advocates for black gays, lesbians, and bisexuals. In his remarks, Robinson argued that, "[t]he struggle of blacks during the civil rights movement of the 1950s and '60s mirrors the battles fought by same-sex couples for equal rights today."

Because they are seen as opposing an issue of civil rights, proponents of heterosexual marriage are often compared to those segregationists in the South who opposed interracial marriage. But such unfounded labels are thrown by the very same people who oppose giving equal marriage rights to other unions. If their analogy to the civil rights movement is correct, they are equally as bigoted for opposing civil rights for bigamous, polygamous, incestuous, and pedophilic relationships.

Race is and should be a specially protected class in our society because it is fundamentally unfair to judge someone by the color of their skin, an immutable characteristic they cannot change, than by their character, something they are entirely responsible for. Sexual orientation, on the other hand, is a behavioral choice that can be unmade. There are numerous former homosexuals, but there are no former black people.

Several years ago proponents of homosexual rights argued that they were born homosexual and therefore couldn't help it. But the science they trumpeted to advance their agenda soon turned out to be junk science and now few proponents of same-sex marriage can be found who rely on it. It is interesting to note that the Iowa Supreme Court didn't even mention, even in passing, that it found gays were born that way and therefore were entitled to the same rights as heterosexuals.

Sexual orientation is a behavior people freely and voluntarily choose to participate in and, therefore, it is not an immutable characteristic entitled to the same protections as race is. It has no comparison with the civil rights movement, which fought for rights specifically guaranteed in the Constitution. The Thirteenth, Fourteenth, and Fifteenth Amendments to the U.S. Constitution were passed in order to protect the recently freed black population after the Civil War.

To compare those who choose to be gay with the struggles of the segregated and trampled upon black man during the civil rights movement is not only disingenuous but also disrespectful. Have gays been kidnapped in their native country, transported in deplorable conditions on ships to a new land, forced to work with only the barest of necessities, and whipped or killed if they attempted to escape? And have homosexuals, upon receiving their freedom from slavery, been subjected to a hundred years of racial prejudice and hatred that prevent them from voting, obtaining an education, and finding good employment?

The answer is a resounding no. Homosexuality has nothing in common with the civil rights movement—it is not an immutable characteristic, it is not a right protected in the constitution, and it's history of "prosecution" pales in comparison with that of the black community.

Even if proponents of same-sex marriage could overcome all this, however, the logical outcome of elevating sexual choice to a civil right is, as referenced earlier, the fact that all sexual choices—whether homosexual, bigamous, polygamous, incestuous, pedophilic, beastious, necrophilca—are constitutionally protected.

If this is a matter of constitutional fairness and equal protection, all similarly situated sexual relationships must be equally protected. Since race is a constitutionally protected right, all races—whether white, black, Hispanic, Asian, etc..—cannot be discriminated against. Likewise, if sexual preference is a constitutional right, every kind of sexual choice must also be protected from discrimination.

In reviewing claims that a state law violates equal protection, courts determine what type of right is at stake and, correspondingly, what type of burden the state must prove to justify its law. Race is one of a few classes of rights in which the courts have held there is slim to no justification for discriminatory laws. Likewise, if sexual choice is truly an extension of the civil rights movement on par with racial discrimination, then there exist few, if any, justifications for laws restricting sexual relations.

The logical outcome of equating gay marriage to the civil rights movement is that all sexual relations are constitutionally protected, and proponents of same-sex marriage who try to limit marriage to only homosexuals but not other unions are simply as bigoted as the rest of us. They are just more hypocritical in doing so.

The Supreme Law
of the Land
April 26, 2009

STARTING AT 8:00 ON THE morning of Monday, April 27th, the Iowa Supreme Court's recent decision legalizing same-sex marriage will go into effect across the state, an action which poses a crises of conscience for many who believe that homosexual marriage is immoral. Already many pastors have publicly announced from their pulpits that they will not perform homosexual marriages in their churches, decisions protected from state interference by the Religion Clause of the First Amendment. And at least one magistrate has stated that he will no longer perform marriages, a discretionary function of his office, in order to avoid presiding over same-sex weddings.

But there are those elected officials who face the conscience-wrenching decision between following their faith or an oath of office which gives them no discretion on the issue. This past week on the floor of the Iowa Senate, Senator Merlin Bartz of Grafton urged Iowans to petition their county recorders to obey the Defense of Marriage Act statute which the Supreme Court struck down rather than follows the Court's decision. Joining his call is the Iowa Family Policy Center, who is encouraging rallies to take place at county recorder's office across the state at 7:30 Monday morning.

The question becomes, therefore, whether elected officials such as county recorders have the ability under our constitutional system of government to ignore court decisions they believe are legally, as well as morally, wrong. As U.S. Chief Justice John Marshall wrote in *Marbury v. Madison* in 1803, "It is emphatically the province and duty of the judicial department to say what the law is…If two laws conflict with each other, the courts must decide that case conformably to the law, disregarding the constitution, or conformably to the constitution, disregarding the law; the court must determine which of these conflicting rules governs the case. This is the very essence of judicial duty."

Nor is the Marshall Court the first to articulate the idea of judicial review. The very first Supreme Court held that it had the power to review laws in *Hylton v. United States*, and numerous state and federal judges affirmed the doctrine of judicial review in the years following the Revolutionary War.

Judicial review—the ability of judges to strike down laws that violate the Constitution—is the very cornerstone of a constitutional democracy, without which majority rule, not the Constitution, becomes the supreme law of the land. As U.S. Supreme Court Justice Joseph Story wrote in his famous Commentaries on the U.S. Constitution, "There can be no security for the minority in a free government, except through the judicial department."

He went on to write, "In their view, the will of the people, as exhibited in the choice of rulers, is to be followed. If the rulers interpret the constitution differently from the judges, the former are to be obeyed...But, is it not at once seen, that this is in fact subverting the constitution? Would it not make the constitution an instrument of flexible and changeable interpretation, and not a settled form of government with fixed limitations...In human government, therefore, there are but two controlling powers; the power of arms, and the power of laws. If the latter are not enforced by the judiciary above all fear, and above all reproach, the former must prevail; and thus lead to the triumph of military over civil institutions."

Though the courts may error and issue decisions that appear to be made "out of judicial whole cloth," their decisions must be obeyed if rights are to be protected and civil order is to exist in our country. Abraham Lincoln recognized this despite his vigorous disagreement with the U.S. Supreme Court's most denounced decision of the 19th century— *Dred Scott v. Sanford* (1857).

Instead of urging elected officials to ignore the Court's decision that held that blacks had no rights and were property that could not be excluded from federal territories, Lincoln systematically exposed the flaws of the Court's reasoning and hoped that the Court would reverse itself in the future. He argued that, "We know the court that has made it has often overruled its own decision, and we shall do what we can to have it overrule this. We offer no resistance to it..."

The Iowa Supreme Court's decision is, for the time being, the supreme law of the land and must be followed by our elected officials. The supreme law of the land can only be changed by means of a constitutional amendment. If elected officials cannot conscientiously follow the Court's ruling because they believe it is wrong morally and/or legally, they should resign their positions in protest. To do otherwise would make every official a Gary Newsom—a law unto themselves—and invite anarchy.

BLIND JUSTICE?

May 2, 2009

THIS PAST WEEK U.S. SUPREME Court Justice David Souter announced that he would be retiring at the end of the present Court's term in June, and Washington's favorite parlor game of guessing who President Obama's nominee to replace him has already begun in earnest. Adding to the speculation on Friday, President Obama reiterated his campaign pledge that he would nominate someone who had empathy.

While empathy is a quality to be admired, it is not something that we should look for in those we appoint to the bench. Empathy is not a judicial philosophy but rather a gut feeling. It is rooting for your favorite character in a movie, or for the underdog sports team to pull the upset. It is, in short, picking who you want to win in any given case.

The problem for judges, however, is they can make an even playing field uneven by ignoring or creating the rules in order to manipulate the outcome they want. The judges are not simply spectators cheering for a particular outcome, but we have entrusted them to enforce the rules of the game much as referee does in sports. To ask our judicial referees to have empathy would be asking them to throw the game in order to obtain a particular outcome. If a sports referee did that, he would, at a minimum, lose his job and may face prosecution and a prison sentence.

Justice is not empathy; justice is blind. Justice is not manipulating the laws so that your favorite litigant may win, but it is enforcing the laws without preference or bias. Lady justice wears a blindfold for a reason— judges are to decide cases based on the law, not on the race, religion, economic status, or favorite color of the parties before them. Above the doors to the Supreme Court are the words, "Equal Justice Under the Law," not "We Will Help You Win if We Like You."

In some cases a majority of Americans may share the justice's empathy in a particular case and applaud the "just" outcome, but there will be just as many cases where we may find ourselves on the other side of the court's empathy. The laws are there to protect us, and once we give judges the power to ignore them for the sake of empathy we no longer can claim their protection.

This point is illustrated by *A Man For All Seasons*, Robert Bolt's famous play about Thomas More. While he was Lord Chancellor of England, Moore's daughter, Margaret, and his son-in-law, Roper, urged him to arrest a man who they considered bad even though he hadn't broken any laws. Margaret said, "Father, that man's bad." More replied, "There's no law against that." Roper responded, "There is! God's law!" More, refusing to ignore the law to play favorites, replied, "Then God can arrest him…The law, Roper, the law. I know what's legal not what's right. And I'll stick to what's legal…For I'm *not* God."

Roper would not concede the point and argued that More would give the Devil the benefit of the doubt. More responded, "Yes.

What would you do? Cut a great road through the law to get after the Devil?" Roper, failing to see the outcome of his empathy, responded, "I'd cut down every law in England to do that!" Moore replied, "Oh?...And when the last law was down and the Devil turns round on you—where would you hide, Roper, the laws all being flat?...Yes, I'd give the Devil the benefit of the law, for my own safety's sake."

Justice Oliver Wendell Holmes, Jr. and Judge Learned Hand were having lunch one day and, according to the story, as Justice Holmes was driving off in his carriage, Hand ran after him crying out, "Do justice, sir, do justice." Holmes stopped his carriage and admonished Hand, "That is not my job. It is my job to apply the law." In dissenting from a case that was decided on empathy rather than the law, Judge Robert Bork wrote, "[W]e administer justice according to the law. Justice in a larger sense, justice according to morality, is for Congress and the President to administer, if they see fit, through the creation of new law."

In the confirmation process to come throughout the summer months, we would do well to remember that justice is served when judges rule on the law and not on their emotions.

Nathan W. Tucker

VETOING THE SUPREME COURT?
May 3, 2009

POLITICAL CAMPAIGNING causes people to say some pretty absurd things in hopes of gaining votes. It always has and it always will. For example, after the Iowa Supreme Court ruled that same-sex marriage was a constitutional right, 2010 gubernatorial candidate Bob Vander Plaats called on Governor Chet Culver to issue an executive order staying the court's ruling until the people had a chance to vote on the issue. As support for his proposition, Vander Plaats refers to a guest op-ed in the Des Moines Register by a Herbert Titus, an attorney and law professor who lives in Virginia.

As precedent for a "veto" of a court's ruling, Mr. Titus cites several historical examples which he claims makes his point. The first example is President Thomas Jefferson, who Titus correctly points out pardoned violators of the infamous Alien & Sedition Act of 1798 even though the law had been upheld as constitutional. Jefferson did not "veto" a mandated order of the court, however, but simply used his constitutionally delegated power of the pardon to, in effect, nullify what he considered to be an unconstitutional law (a law which was repealed shortly after he took office).

Secondly, Titus argues that President Andrew Jackson "vetoed" the Supreme Court when he vetoed a bill renewing the charter of the National Bank, a bank the Supreme Court had held to be constitutional in *McCulloch v. Maryland*. But once again this only reveals a president acting within his constitutional powers to end a law he believed was unconstitutional. The veto power, as with the pardon power, are clearly enumerated powers given to the chief executive under the Constitution and were not, in these two examples, used to impede a mandate of the Supreme Court.

The third example Titus points to is President Abraham Lincoln. By not seeking a constitutional amendment following the

Supreme Court's decision in *Dred Scott* that held that blacks had no rights and could not be excluded from the new federal territories, Titus jumps to the erroneous conclusion, without citing any supporting statements by Lincoln, that Lincoln knew that the chief executive could ignore the Supreme Court's ruling.

But Lincoln did in fact favor a constitutional amendment overruling *Dred Scott*, stating in his First Inaugural Address that, "I should under existing circumstances favor rather than oppose a fair opportunity being afforded the people to act on it." He even went on to state his preference for the manner in which the Constitution should be amended.

Concerning the *Dred Scott* decision itself, Lincoln in his First Inaugural Address stated that, "[I]t is obviously possible that such decision may be erroneous in any given case, still the evil effect following it, being limited to that particular case, with the chance that it may be over-ruled, and never become a precedent for other cases, can better be borne than could the evils of a different practice [i.e., disobeying the Court's ruling]." Here Lincoln acknowledged that Supreme Court decisions were binding precedent, but he hoped that the Court would overrule itself before that occurred.

Though Mr. Titus' examples do not support his proposition that the chief executive can "veto" the Supreme Court, there are two other historical precedents that address this issue directly. The first example is President Jackson, who purportedly reacted to the Supreme Court's decision in *Worcester v. Georgia*, which held that Georgia's laws violating federal treaties with the Cherokee nation were unconstitutional, by stating "Well, [Chief Justice] John Marshall has made his decision, now let him enforce it."

Even if Jackson did make this statement, something which remains disputed, it unfortunately no more helps Titus than his previous examples because the Court's decision was directed at the state of Georgia and did not order Jackson or the federal government to do anything.

The second example is President Lincoln, who ignored Chief Justice Roger Taney's decision in the *Merryman* case. Shortly after his inauguration in 1861, Lincoln faced the prospect of the nation's capital situated just across the Potomac River from the Confederacy and cut off from Union troops by secessionist sympathizers in Maryland who cut telegraph lines and destroyed railroad tracks and bridges.

Given this dire situation, on April 27, 1861, President Lincoln authorized, on his own authority as commander in chief, the suspension of the right of habeas corpus along any military line between Philadelphia and Washington. John Merryman, a Maryland secessionist who was arrested and confined to Fort McHenry, petitioned Taney to hear his case. Taney ruled in his favor, holding that Lincoln's actions were illegal and that only Congress had the explicit constitutional authority to suspend habeas corpus in times of insurrection. President Lincoln ignored Taney's ruling and not only continued to enforce the suspension of habeas corpus in Maryland, but extended it in September 1862 to include anyone confined by the military authority.

But this single example of a chief executive who "vetoed" a court's ruling in a time when the nation's very survival was at stake doesn't justify a president or governor taking the same action today. Lincoln justified his defiance of the court's ruling on the grounds that a rebellion "in nearly one-third of the States" had subverted the "whole of the laws...are all the laws, *but one*, to go unexecuted, and the government itself to go to pieces, lest that one be violated?"

No such emergency exists today to justify a chief executive "vetoing" a court's decision. In the absence, therefore, of support in the Constitution or historic practice, the proposition of Vander Plaats and Titus that a president or governor can ignore a court order is a dangerous and illegitimate theory that should rightfully be denounced.

Nathan W. Tucker

FRANKENSTEIN

May 10, 2009

IN ADDITION TO HIS GUEST opinion editorial in The Des Moines Register, Mr. Titus wrote yet another in The Sioux City Journal on behalf of Vander Platt's argument that the chief executive has the authority to "veto" a court decision. The reason, presumably, for two different op-eds is that, when a paper prints an op-ed, they have the exclusive rights to it. So in order to get two different papers to publish his op-eds, Titus had to write two different versions.

But his op-eds are quite similar—in the piece that appeared in The Sioux City Journal he introduces the concept of the governor as the "chief executive power" who has the constitutional duty to prevent a court's illegal decision from being carried out. In the column which was published in The Des Moines Register, Titus provides presidential precedent that he claims supports his proposition.

As has already been noted, none of Titus' examples actually involved a chief executive who acted to prevent a court decision he believed was unconstitutional. Two additional examples were also explored, but one only expressed a presidential sentiment about a Supreme Court case addressed to the State of Georgia, and the other, though directly on point, occurred when the nation itself was at peril during the early months of the Civil War.

Since Titus has failed to cite any historical precedent for his proposition, or any statements by the Constitutional Framers supporting his thesis, his argument should be treated with a great deal of skepticism. But when fully explored, Titus' constitutional framework actually creates a Frankenstein—a chief executive who is a law unto himself with the ability to say what is constitutional and what isn't. In order to provide a check against the threat of judicial tyranny, Titus paves the way for a return of absolute authority held by one man, be he a president or a governor.

As previously discussed, the very cornerstone of a constitutional democracy is an independent judiciary with the power to strike down laws that violate the Constitution. If the chief executive can refuse to enforce those decisions, than the law begins and ends with him for there no longer exists any check on his power. Even if the legislature could exert some influence over him (a doubtful proposition given that he now has unlimited authority over the military), the Constitution would simply be a result of a power struggle between the two branches and no longer a check on either.

Titus' argument is an example of the means justifying convenient (and political?) ends. It is born out of conservative frustration over decades of judicial decisions it believes not only has no basis in the Constitution, but usurps its original meaning. Ever since the Warren Court, conservatives have had to swallow decisions giving criminal defendants unprecedented protections in the name of the Bill of Rights, that mandated abortion in the name of reproductive rights, legalized pornography in the name of free speech, that took God out of the public forum in the name of the First Amendment, and that held sodomy was protected under the rubric of privacy.

These are just a few of the things that have turned conservative hearts against the judiciary. But to achieve his goal of reversing these decisions by executive "veto," Titus would create a constitutional framework that leaves rights protected only by the will of one man—the chief executive. In order to achieve conservative ends, he has created a means by which conservatives causes can come to an end.

For example, there is no power left under Titus' theory to prevent the chief executive from enforcing an executive order mandating that pastors can no longer say anything discriminating against homosexuals. The court may (rightly) decide that such an executive order is unconstitutional, but if the chief executive has the authority to decide what is constitutional and what isn't, it really doesn't make a difference what the court says.

Likewise, if a chief executive would take it upon himself to decide that, not only should pornography be banned, but so should all religious media, there is no longer any constitutional check on his actions.

In giving the chief executive the power to decide when the courts have issued an unconstitutional decision, we have removed the only constitutional check on the chief executive's actions and reduced the law to the force of arms. By creating a hero to impede liberal judicial activism, we have created a monster that could quite easily turn on us.

Nathan W. Tucker

CHECKING JUDICIAL TYRANNY
May 10, 2009

HOW DO WE SOLVE A PROBLEM like the tyranny of the judiciary? People from every corner of the political spectrum have their own lists of grievances against an activist judiciary. Liberals decry it for not granting enough "rights," while conservatives believe it has created too many rights that are not found in the text of the Constitution. Issues such as abortion, sexual orientation, eminent domain, religious freedom, and, yes, even presidential elections, are seen as being usurped from public deliberation by robed tyrants.

But the problem of "checking" the judiciary is difficult because, as Alexander Hamilton noted in Federalist Papers No. 78, the independence of the judiciary is essential in a constitutional democracy. Writing in May of 1788 to encourage the ratification of the U.S. Constitution, Hamilton argued that constitutional limitations, "can be preserved in practice no other way than through the medium of the courts of justice; whose duty it must be to declare all acts contrary to the manifest tenor of the constitution void. Without this, all the reservations of particular rights or privileges would amount to nothing."

In refuting claims that this power of judicial review established the judiciary above the other two co-equal branches of government, Hamilton pointed out that it simply means that, "the power of the people is superior to both [the judiciary and legislature]; and that where the will of the legislature declared in its statutes, stands in opposition to that of the people declared in the constitution, the judges ought to be governed by the later, rather than the former."

Since "the courts of justice are to be considered as the bulwarks of a limited constitution against legislative [and executive] encroachments," Hamilton and his fellow Constitutional Framers sought to strengthen the judiciary against the other two branches by giving judges life tenure and ensuring their salary cannot be decreased. Those who gave us our Constitution were concerned that, as the weakest and least dangerous branch of government, the judiciary would be overpowered by the legislature and chief executive.

But little could the Framers have imagine a day in which there exists a judicial theory to justify any and everything under the sun. Ideas such as substantive due process, a living constitution, critical race theory, and feminist jurisprudence has made the words of the "fundamental law" putty in the hands of judges who act with, as President Obama termed it, empathy. The judicial nomination process is no longer a means to test the qualities of a particular nominee, but to see if they will promise us everything on our "constitutional wish list."

Does there, therefore, exist a solution to this dilemma of "judicial lawmaking" that will simultaneously protect the independence of the judiciary (and, as a consequence, of our rights) and yet at the same time serve as a bulwark against encroachments by those who we have entrusted to interpret the constitution? Hamilton tried to come up with a solution in Federalist No. 78, noting that, "[t]o avoid an arbitrary discretion in the courts, it is indispensable that they should be bound down by strict rules and precedents, which serve to define and point out their duty in every particular case that comes before them." Through the centuries, however, precedent has often failed to serve as a check on the judiciary.

Several attempts have been made to reign in the judiciary through the appointment and impeachment processes. In 1805, Jeffersonian Democrats attempted to impeach U.S. Supreme Court Justice Samuel Chase in an effort to attack the constitutional jurisprudence of the Federalist Marshall Court. The attempt failed, however, because enough Senators concurred with Chase's defense that "[o]ur property, our liberty, our lives can only be protected and secured by [independent] judges." Impeachment as a tool of reigning in the judiciary soon becomes a witch hunt by which that branch becomes persecuted and devoid of any semblance of the independence necessary to serve as a bulwark of protection.

In February, 1937, President Franklin Roosevelt had had enough of the Supreme Court's refusal to go along with his New Deal program and decided to manipulate the nomination process to "pack" the Supreme Court. In order to give himself a majority on the Supreme Court, FDR proposed that the President could appoint another judge for every federal judge who was over seventy and had not yet retired. The nation was appalled at the president's audacious assault on the judiciary, however, and the proposal never made it out of the Senate Judiciary Committee.

In the weeks after the Iowa Supreme Court struck down that State's Defense of Marriage Act, tentative gubernatorial candidate Bob Vander Plaats and his trusted sidekick Herbert Titus have proposed that the chief executive, the governor has a constitutional obligation to refuse to implement a judicial decision he considers unconstitutional. The idea was also floated by an Iowa Senator that the State's county recorders had an obligation to refuse to allow homosexuals to marry in their counties. Such theories have been shown elsewhere to not only be unconstitutional but also dangerous.

In the end, the only satisfactory process by which erroneous judicial interpretations of the people's will, as expressed in the Constitution, can be remedied without dangerously emasculating the judiciary is by amending the fundamental law to rightfully express the people's will. In a democracy, We the People say what the law is and, if it has been misinterpreted by our judicial stewards, we must undertake the process of correcting that error by means of a constitutional amendment.

Such a process, however, is long and cumbersome and has yet to repeal any acts of judicial abuse and tyranny. The process is purposefully meant to be difficult so that the temporary passions of a majority will not make things worse by an ill-conceived amendment that has not been fully deliberated. But in light of an increasingly active judiciary and the corresponding loss of public faith in its decisions, it is perhaps time to amend the amendment process itself.

At both the state and federal level, therefore, the amendment process should be modified to allow citizens the ability to place a constitutional amendment directly on the ballot for voters to consider and ratify. Before it can be placed on the ballot, the proposed amendment must meet a specified number of valid signatures in order to show that it has sufficient public support.

In order to ensure that there has been sufficient time for thoughtful deliberation by a public not caught up in the heat of the moment, it must be passed by voters in two election cycles within five years of each other. If a greater span than five years is allowed, it becomes much more likely that ratification will be driven by two sudden bursts of public opinion rather than a deliberative process.

At the state level, such an amendment would become law if approved by a simple majority of ballots cast in two separate elections. To avoid sectionalism and majorities in one part of the country from pushing through an amendment on its reluctant neighbors, the process at the federal level would retain the current requirement that, in order to be ratified, an amendment must be approved, by simple majorities, by three-fourths of the states.

By use of such ballot initiatives, We the People can ensure that we have the final say over what the fundamental law is without eroding the ability of the judiciary to serve as a bulwark of our rights and liberties.

THE IOWA MARRIAGE AMENDMENT IS NOT...
Spring 2004/Updated May 13, 2009

THE   IOWA   MARRIAGE
Amendment reads: "Only marriage between a man and a woman is valid or recognized in this state."

1. ...discriminatory. The language of the Iowa Marriage Amendment (IMA) does not discriminate against homosexuals as a class; it merely prevents *all* unmarried couples or groups from enjoying the legal status of marriage. The IMA no more discriminates against homosexuals than it does bigamous, polygamous, incestuous, and bestious couples. Today it is homosexuals who claims discrimination, 120 years ago bigamous and polygamous Mormon couples would have cried "discrimination," and in another 120 years incestuous and bestious couples may allege "discrimination." The IMA does not differentiate between the unmarried couples and groups that threaten marriage; rather, it

53

protects that sacred and essential institution from them all.

Homosexual activists attempt to portray their movement akin to that of the civil rights movement of the 1950's and 60's. But the civil rights movement was not just a movement for equal rights for black people but for people of *all* races. There was no moral or logical way for the movement to claim equal rights for one ethnic minority while denying it to all others. But that is exactly what the homosexual movement is doing; claiming that marriage laws discriminate against them while refusing to raise a voice on behalf of all other couples or groups who are also prohibited from marrying. The claim of discrimination is a sham by the homosexual movement, intended to play on the hearts of Iowans while in reality it is at its very core hypocritical.

2. ...the first time a constitution has been amended to take away someone's rights. First, the IMA does not take away the rights of any unmarried couple or group because in the entire history of our state they have never been entitled to the rights, benefits, protections, and responsibilities of marriage. Any exclusive legal category naturally excludes those outside that category from enjoying the legal rights of that category, but to claim that this thereby takes away people's rights and is somehow immoral would naturally void all classifications, such as tax incentives and credits, made by the legislature.

Secondly, assuming *arguendo* that the IMA does take away rights, so did the 13th Amendment to the U.S. Constitution which took away the "property" rights of slave owners estimated at a total value of $1,576,206,000 (not adjusted for inflation). Few, if any, would argue today that the 13th Amendment was illegitimate because it took away slave owner's rights.

3. ...just "legislating morality" in order to prevent people from doing what they want even though they don't hurt anyone. There is nothing wrong with legislation based solely on the basis of a people's moral attitudes in the absence of a "victim." If such legislation was inappropriate, laws against suicide, assisted suicide, bodily mutilation, illegal drugs, bigamy, polygamy, incest, prostitution, adultery, fornication, bestiality, necrophilia, and eating or otherwise mutilating dead people would also be inappropriate.

Some argue that a constitution should not be amended to enshrine a social policy. But the U.S. Constitution already contains many existing provisions which already deal with social issues, such as those which protect the rights of religious liberty, free speech, political association, equality for all races, and the right to vote to those over 18 regardless of race or gender.

4. ...enshrining into the constitution old-fashioned bigoted notions of marriage analogous to now disregarded views of marriage and the family, such as prohibitions on interracial marriage and restrictions on women's property rights, women's right to vote, and the ability of the wife to keep her maiden name. While it is true that these and other legal notions of marriage—such as age, capacity to contract, and the specific degree of consanguinity—have varied from state to state and time to time, there have been three constant, unchanging norms of marriage in Western civilization over the past millennia—monogamy, heterosexuality, and a requisite degree of consanguinity.

Homosexual activists, however, would like to replace the norm of heterosexuality by redefining marriage as a "loving, intimate relationship."   The Iowa Supreme Court appears to have adopted such a redefinition, holding that marriage restrictions must be justified   by   "exceedingly   persuasive justification(s)."   The consequences of this redefinition, however, are two-fold. First, there is no logical way to stop it from bringing other similarly situated monogamous and non-related couples—those   who   are   bestious   and pedophiliac—into its orbit. Secondly, there is no logical way to stop it from sweeping the other two norms—monogamy and a requisite degree of consanguinity—before its path and thereby legalizing bigamous, polygamous, incestuous, and who-knows-what other marriages.

This new "love and let love" understanding of marriage with "acceptance and understanding for [those] who choose to love differently than the majority" is, in reality, a free for all in which the imagination is the only limit to what a marriage is, thereby degenerating marriage into a hollow, meaningless, and insignificant institution.

5. ...the work of right-wing radicals. The IMA is supported by a broad range of organizations and individuals, including leaders representing virtually every religion in Iowa as well as those who do not subscribe to a religious faith at all. People from every walk of life believe that marriage is between one man and one woman. Polls have consistently shown that the vast majority of Iowans, regardless of party, faith, or background, support the passage of the IMA.

6. ...annulling current gay marriages. The validity and recognition of all marriages in Iowa would be limited to one man and one woman, including past and future marriages, as well as marriages from other states or countries. The rights and obligations of same-sex couple who obtained marriage licenses before the IMA passes will be up to the courts to decide.

7. ...unconstitutional.   First, the courts cannot declare the IMA to be unconstitutional.   The constitution is the supreme law of the land because it is the people's will. The constitution, as fundamental law, controls the courts, who will be obligated to uphold traditional marriage. Even the liberal California Supreme Court, which had earlier ruled in favor of gay marriage, later upheld the California Marriage Amendment by recognizing the right of the people to change the Constitution and, thereby, the court's prior ruling.

Secondly, it is perfectly proper for the people to tell the court when they got it wrong. Just because the court misinterpreted the Constitution, it does not mean that the people cannot amend the Constitution to remedy that interpretation. Both the 11th and 13th Amendments were passed in direct response to Supreme Court decisions that the American people felt were wrongly decided. The courts do not have the ultimate say over the people's will as contained in the Constitution; the people do through the amendment process. We the People are, ultimately, the supreme law of the land and we should not abrogate our power to the courts when they get it wrong.

****

Thus stripped of all these rhetorical trappings, opponents of the IMA have not offered a single, solid, logical argument why the majority of Iowans should not pass the IMA which, until they do, makes one wonder why anyone should listen to them.

AMENDING INALIENABLE RIGHTS
May 31, 2009

IN AN EDITORIAL ON MAY 29th entitled "Gay-marriage ruling less than it appears," The Des Moines Register argued that, in effect, We the People cannot change our constitution via the amendment process to reverse an earlier court ruling. Last week the California Supreme Court held that Proposition 8, passed by a majority of voters in 2008, was in fact constitutional. Prop 8 amended the California Constitution to declare that only heterosexual marriage is valid in that state, overruling an earlier ruling by the California Supreme Court which held that gays had a right to marry.

The Register, however, argues that the California Supreme Court limited the amendment in such a way as to avoid changing it's "earlier holding that gay couples cannot be denied the same constitutional rights that heterosexual couples enjoy."   The Register hypothesizes that, if the court did not limit the amendment's reading, it "likely would have struck down the amendment entirely because it would have violated the equal-protection clause of…the state…constitution[]" as previously interpreted by that court.

Stating that "this line of reasoning has implications for Iowa," the Register argues that, if the Iowa Constitution were amended to prohibit homosexual marriage, the Iowa Supreme Court would strike it down as unconstitutional because "[a]n amendment that would strip same-sex couples of [marriage] rights could not be squared with [the court's] earlier ruling."

Among the many problems with the Register's analysis of the California Supreme Court's ruling is that the Court explicitly rejected the argument made by the Register. In its opinion, the court ruled:

> [T]he Attorney General maintains that "Proposition 8 should be invalidated even if it is deemed to amend the Constitution because it abrogates fundamental rights

protected by article 1 without a compelling interest."...

[But] the "inalienable" nature of a constitutional right never has been understood to preclude the adoption of a *constitutional amendment* that limits or restricts the scope or application of such a right....

Accordingly, there is no basis for suggesting that the inalienable rights set forth in article 1, section 1, and the other provisions of the Declaration of Rights, are of a higher order than—and thus exempt from—the people's right to "alter or reform" the Constitution through either the legislative or the initiative constitutional amendment process. Indeed, a review of the current version of the constitutional provisions contained within article 1's Declaration of Rights demonstrates that modification of such rights through the amendment process has occurred throughout our state's history. (The emphasis in original.)

It is bad enough that the Register ignored the court's rejection of its argument, but the Register perpetuated its wrong by misconstruing the court's opinion to the people of Iowa in such a way as to support the opposite of what it said. So much for journalistic, or editorial, integrity.

Furthermore, the Register's argument reveals a fundamental misunderstanding of the nature of our constitutional democracy. The supreme law of the land is not simply the Constitution, but the will of the people as embodied in the Constitution. We the People are the creators of our Constitution, and we established in that document the procedures whereby we can amend or alter that document as we see fit.

If the people choose to exercise their right to amend their constitution, the courts are powerless to stop them. As the California Supreme Court noted in its ruling, to do otherwise "would exceed the well-established and time-honored limits of the judicial role were we to take it upon ourselves to fashion such a restriction upon the present and future right of the people to determine the content of the Constitution that governs our state."

As the court noted, several well-respected commentators concur that We the People are our own rulers. Liberal constitutional thinker Lawrence Tribe wrote, "allowing the judiciary to pass on the merits of constitutional amendments would unequivocally subordinate the amendment process to the legal system it is intended to override and would thus gravely threaten the integrity of the entire structure." Another commentator argued, "To empower the courts not simply to review the procedures whereby amendments were adopted but also to void amendments on the basis of their substantive content would surely threaten the notion of a government founded on the consent of the governed."

Finally, the Register's argument is wrong in practice, as both the 11th, 13th, 14th, and 15th Amendments were passed in direct response to Supreme Court decisions that the American people felt were wrongly decided. In fact, the 13th Amendment took away "inalienable property rights" of slave owners that were estimated at a total value of $1,576,206,000 (not adjusted for inflation).

Contrary to what The Des Moines Register may say about its ruling, the California Supreme Court's opinion clearly holds that We the People may amend our fundamental will as reflected in the Constitution in any way we so choose, and no court may stop us. And if they should try, they should be impeached. And any editorial board that advocates such a position under the guise of knowingly misconstruing a court decision should be thrown out.

DIVIDED WE FAIL

June 21, 2009

CONSERVATIVE LEADERS IN Iowa are divided over the direction they should take in response to the Iowa Supreme Court's ruling that held that Iowa Defense of Marriage Act (DOMA) was unconstitutional. To date, the division within the Republican Party has not been between moderates and conservatives over whether a marriage amendment to the Iowa Constitution should ban civil unions in addition to gay marriage. Rather, the division is turning conservative against conservative and threatens the success of any effort to reverse the court's ruling.

The debate is ostensibly over tactics— whether we should have an executive order "pausing" the court's decision, whether we should push for in-state residency requirements before migrant gay couples can marry in Iowa, impeachment of the justices, and/or whether we should push for a marriage amendment. But this rift over tactics reflects a deeper and more fundamental divide among conservatives over the nature of our constitutional democracy.

The "purists," represented by Bob Vander Plaats, the Iowa Family Policy Center, and Steve Deace of WHO Radio, argue that enough is enough and it is time to stand up to unconstitutional decisions by the judiciary. They argue that the court violated the constitutional mandate of separation of powers because it made law from the bench and found a "constitutional right" out of judicial whole cloth.

Therefore, they argue, the ruling is unconstitutional and the other two co-equal branches of government not only have the power but the duty to refuse to implement it. (The focus has primarily been on the executive rather than the legislature, quite possibly because the "purists" have a favorite horse (i.e., Vander Plaats) in the 2010 governor's race.) They argue that the DOMA is still good law, that the governor should enforce it, the marriage forms should never have been changed, and the county recorders should not be handing out "sodomy licenses."

The crux of the argument is that now is the time to stand up to an activist, liberal judiciary and tell them that they do not have the power of judicial review; that they cannot overrule the will of the majority. From the "purist's" perspective, anything short of refusing to acknowledge, enforce, and obey the court's decision is an acknowledgment of its legitimacy. Therefore, we should not pursue such options as residency requirements and even a constitutional amendment because that would be an acknowledgment that the court had the authority to make its decision in the first place. In fact, the IFPC has refused help from national pro-family groups unless they agree to work within their "purist" parameters, something which no organization has yet to do.

As a practical matter, however, the success of this strategy is tied to one man— Vander Plaats. Whether directly or indirectly, intentionally or unintentionally, the fight for traditional marriage in Iowa for these "purists" begins and ends with the election of Vander Plaats to the governor's mansion in 2010. If he should lose either the primary or the general election, the "purists" run out of options. If they are able to find another standard-bearer, the next opportunity for their candidate to win the governorship is 2014, by which time the public outcry over the court's decision will have diminished to a whimper. And any attempt to push for a marriage amendment or residency requirements after a Vander Plaats loss will strike of expedient, politically motivated hypocrisy.

Additionally, the "puritans" have, as all puritans eventually do, become arrogant and intolerant of those who disagree with them. On Deace's radio show they are called "left of the left" and "constitution never," and any governor of any party (Romney, Schwarrzenegger, or Culver) who refuses to disobey a court order should be imprisoned. Instead of seeking to convince, persuade, and unite conservatives behind their agenda, they lambaste those who take a different approach as unfaithful to the constitution. This only deepens the fissures within the pro-marriage movement and threatens any chance at unity and victory.

Finally, the approach taken by the "purists" will never succeed because it is fundamentally wrong, and the majority of the electorate—conservative, liberal, and moderate—know it. That is why there hasn't been a single county recorder who has refused to issue gay marriage licenses, or gubernatorial candidate other than Vander Plaats who has promised to issue an executive order preventing the implementation of the court's ruling. The people of Iowa know that, as Congressmen Steve King noted in an editorial in The Des Moines Register, "using the rule of law to reverse the Iowa Supreme Court's decision by amending the Constitution is the only way to uphold it and confer legitimacy on the process-something the decision itself lacks."

It is past time that pro-family groups organize and unite on a common course of action to preserve marriage in Iowa—a constitutional amendment. We have the numbers to easily pass it in both the Iowa General Assembly and the electorate if it ever came up for a vote. So let us put aside the name calling and ideological differences and focus on obtaining the achievable for the sake of our common cause. It is time we remember the words of Lincoln that a house divided among itself cannot stand.

CONSTITUTIONAL CONVENTION—PROMISE OR MAYHEM?
February 3, 2010

GIVEN THE UNWILLINGNESS

of Democratic leaders to allow a marriage amendment to the Iowa Constitution to come to the floor in either chamber of the General Assembly, the question has been raised as to the practicality and the wisdom of pursuing a constitutional amendment by another procedure—the constitutional convention.

The Promise:

The Iowa Constitution provides two methods by which it can be amended. The first and most common procedure is for a majority in both the Iowa House and Senate to pass the proposed amendment in two consecutive terms of the General Assembly. The word *term* should not be confused with a *session* of the Iowa legislature. The word *term* refers to the period between general elections in Iowa when new legislatures are voted in, while the word

73

session refers to a particular period when the legislature is actually convened.

For example, the latest term of the Iowa General Assembly began when it first convened after the 2008 elections, and the next one will begin the first time it convenes after the 2010 elections. The current session, however, of the General Assembly began on January 11th when it convened for its annual meeting and it will, tentatively, end March 31st.

This distinction is important because, if the marriage amendment is passed by both chambers this year, it must be ratified again next term which, fortunately, is also next year. But if, however, the amendment is not passed this year, it has to be passed in either the 2011 or 2012 session and in either the 2013 or 2014 sessions before it can even be presented to the Iowa voters for ratification.

This process is long and laborious and, given the Democratic majorities in both chambers of the General Assembly, seems doubtful of producing a marriage amendment in Iowa. Because the problem of elected representatives ignoring the will of a majority of their constituents is not new, however, the Iowa Constitution provides an alternative procedure which bypasses the legislature in amending the Constitution—a constitutional convention.

This process is described in Article X, Section 3 of the Iowa Constitution:

> At the general election to be held in the year one thousand nine hundred and seventy, and in each tenth year thereafter, and also at such times as the general assembly may, by law, provide, the question, "Shall there be a convention to revise the constitution, and propose amendment or amendments to same?" shall be decided by the electors qualified to vote for members of the general assembly; and in case a majority of electors so qualified, voting at such election, for and against such proposition, shall decide in favor of a convention for such purpose, the general assembly, at its next session, shall provide by law for the election of delegates to such convention, and for submitting the results of said convention to the people, in such manner and at such

times as the general assembly shall provide; and if the people shall approve and ratify such amendment or amendments by a majority of the electors qualified to vote for members of the general assembly, voting thereon, such amendment or amendments shall become a part of the constitution of this state. If two or more amendments shall be submitted at the same time, they shall be submitted in such a manner that electors may vote for or against each such amendment separately.

Since 2010 is a "tenth year thereafter," voters will have a chance this year to vote on whether or not a constitutional convention shall be held to amend the existing constitution. On its face, this procedure appears to be much simpler and much more attainable than the traditional process of amending the Constitution via the legislature.

What About the Mayhem?:

However, there are several serious objections to pursuing this option. The first is that while this process isn't dependent upon the approval of an unresponsive and derelict majority in the General Assembly, that same majority has the responsibility of deciding the process by which delegates are chosen to the constitutional convention. Hence, the argument goes, the Democratic majority will draw the districts from which delegates are chosen in such a way as to ensure they retain a majority in the convention.

While this is a viable concern, I think the concerns over drawing delegate districts are overblown for several reasons. For instance, any other scheme for drawing delegate districts than using existing districts for state legislatures (either senate and/or house) is extremely problematic because of constitutional issues. Because the last time the General Assembly tried to draw the lines up itself it was found to be unconstitutional, it delegated the job to the nonpartisan Legislative Service Bureau.

Therefore, I anticipate the General Assembly to simply utilize the existing state senate districts as delegate districts as they did for the 1857 constitutional convention in order to avoid any legal challenges. Even if, however, the General Assembly tried to gerrymander the delegate districts, I have enough faith in the people in this climate of outrage at politicians, tea parties, and Republicans winning in Massachusetts to elect responsible delegates who will abide by the will of their constituents and not the wishes of Democratic party leaders Senator Mike Gronstal and Speaker Pat Murphy.

A second objection to a constitutional convention is that it would, in essence, open Pandora's Box—anything and everything could be proposed at the convention. Conservatives would come with their wish lists of items such as a marriage amendment, tax and budget reform, gun rights, and gambling, while liberals would champion such causes as union rights, environmental regulation, and health care reform.

While this is certainly a plausible scenario, whatever amendment(s) the constitutional convention produces must be voted upon by the people before it is ratified. I have enough trust in the people that they will reject any liberal amendment. Furthermore, not to discourage my fellow conservatives, only the marriage amendment will likely be ratified by the people as it alone has a huge majority behind it.

A third objection is premised on the first two—that the Democratic Party will manipulate the delegate districts to elect a majority and, once seated, they will seek to throw out the entire existing constitution and replace it with some sinister but yet undefined constitution. Though constitutional conventions have been known to do this (the U.S. Constitutional Convention, for instance, proposed an entirely new constitution rather than simply amend the Articles of Confederation for which it was nominally elected to do), what evil constitution will they seek to replace the existing one with?

I see liberal amendments as a much more attainable goal for liberals than an entire scrapping of the whole constitution, but I again put my faith in the people to reject either. Though left to their own devices Democrats would doubtless seek to create much mischief, their fear of the electorate, especially in this environment, will help restrain this tendency. Last April they dared conservatives to pursue a constitutional amendment, little realizing that at the time the Democratic Party's popularity had already crested and they were about to taking a beating at the polls. Now, they have enough to worry about just to get reelected without attempting much large-scale change in the Constitution.

A fourth objection appears to concern the issue of amendments—that a conservative amendment (i.e., the marriage amendment) may be joined with a liberal one (i.e., health care reform). But this is specifically prohibited under Title Ten of the Constitution, which requires amendments to be voted on individually. And as can be seen from Section 29 of Article Three of the Constitution, each amendment can only embrace one subject. Therefore, an amendment concerning the subject of marriage, for instance, cannot also deal with the subject of health care reform.

Interestingly, the odd argument has been raised that a constitutional convention can ignore this prohibition because its sole purpose is to amend or repeal the constitution. Such an argument, however, appears to put the cart before the horse—even if the constitutional convention wanted to propose an amendment (or a new constitution) that would repeal this prohibition, the existing Constitution remains in effect until the new amendment is voted on by the people.

A constitutional convention does not become a "living constitution" unto itself simply because it can repeal the existing constitution. For instance, the Articles of Confederation remained in effect with the full force of law until the U.S. Constitution was ratified by the 9th state (the minimum required for ratification). It is only when the proposed amendments are approved by the voters that they become law.

The Solution:

Though mayhem appears plausible but unrealistic, conservatives should not fear advocating for a constitutional convention. With that said, however, mayhem is best kept at bay by having a sound, long-term strategy—making the sole purpose of the constitutional convention to amend the Iowa Constitution to create a third procedure by which it could be amended: a ballot initiative whereby citizens can directly propose constitutional amendments without reliance on the legislature or resort to potentially opening Pandora's Box with a constitutional convention.

This strategy serves two purposes. First, if this is the entire purpose of a constitutional convention, it takes the fear and wild speculation out of the process. Conservatives don't have to fret that liberals will highjack the convention and steamroll a liberal constitutional remake, nor will liberals have to fear the same about conservatives. It is a willingness to agree to disagree by recognizing that a constitutional convention is not the most appropriate forum for such explosive and controversial issues. In this political environment, Democrats may well find it hard to be reelected unless they pledge to only seek this one amendment at the convention rather than pursue a liberal agenda.

Second, while this would mean an additional wait of a few years before a marriage amendment is placed on the ballot for the people's vote, it is well worth the wait. For the issue is not simply the definition of marriage in Iowa, but the problem of judicial activism, and there is no other remedy to unconstitutional judicial decisions than to provide individuals with the ability to quickly trump the court's decision by amending the Constitution. It is only then can we become a country in which we truly are sovereign.

The following is my proposed amendment to the Iowa Constitution to allow for ballot initiatives:

Article X
Amendments to the Constitution

Ballot initiative. Section 4. The initiative is the power of the electors to propose amendments to the Constitution and to adopt or reject them.

(a) An initiative measure may be proposed by presenting to the Secretary of State a petition that sets forth the text of the proposed amendment to the Constitution and is certified to have been signed by a number of electors in each one-half of the congressional districts of the state, and of the state as a whole, equal in number to 15 percent of the votes cast in each of such districts respectively and in the state as a whole for all candidates for Governor at the last gubernatorial election.

(b) The initiative measure shall have been signed by the petitioning electors not more than twenty-four months preceding the next general election and shall be filed with the Secretary of State at least 120 days before the next general election.

(c) The Secretary of State shall upon its receipt determine, as provided by law, the validity and sufficiency of the signatures on the petition, and make an official announcement thereof at least 60 days prior to next general election. The Secretary of State shall then submit the measure at the next general election after it qualifies.

(d) Such proposed amendment, existing provisions of the constitution which would be altered or abrogated thereby, and the question as it shall appear on the ballot shall be published in full as provided by law. Copies of such publication shall be posted in each polling place and furnished to news media as provided by law.

(e) The ballot to be used in such election shall contain a statement of the purpose of the proposed amendment, expressed in not more than 100 words, exclusive of caption. Such statement of purpose and caption shall be prepared by the Secretary of State, and shall consist of a true and impartial statement of the purpose of the amendment in such language as shall create no prejudice for or against the proposed amendment.

(f) If the initiative measure is approved by a majority of electors qualified to vote for members of the general assembly, voting thereon, in two of the last three general elections, such amendment or amendments shall become part of the constitution of this state.

(g) An initiative measure embracing more than one subject may not be submitted to the electors or have any effect.

(h) An initiative measure may not include or exclude any political subdivision of the State from the application or effect of its provisions based upon approval or disapproval of the initiative measure, or based upon the casting or a specified percentage of votes in favor of the measure, by the electors of that political subdivision.

(i) An initiative measure may not contain alternative or cumulative provisions wherein one or more of those provisions would become law depending upon the casting of a specified percentage of votes for or against the measure.

Originally published in *The Iowa Republican* on February 6, 2010.

ANSWERING THE CRITICS
OF A BALLOT INITIATIVE
February 7, 2010

RECENTLY I WROTE IN FAVOR of amending the Iowa Constitution at a constitutional convention so as to allow Iowans the ability to propose constitutional amendments by way of a ballot initiative. This proposal was in response to an ongoing discussion among conservatives over the prudence and practicality of using a constitutional convention to pass a marriage amendment in Iowa if the General Assembly failed to vote one out of the legislature for the people's vote.

There are several understandable and viable concerns over the use of a constitutional convention which were addressed in my earlier article. But my proposal for a ballot initiative as a two-fold means to (i) keep the lid on Pandora's Box at such a convention and (ii) check judicial activism aroused concerns of its own with claims, among other things, that it was liberal populism in disguise.

Though the ballot initiative was introduced and enjoyed the height of its popularity during the Progressive Era, my proposal is anything but progressive. The traditional process of amending the constitution through legislative initiative is long and cumbersome and, with the sole exception of the 13th Amendment which overturned *Dred Scott*, has yet to repeal any acts of judicial activism. The process is purposefully meant to be difficult so that the temporary passions of a majority will not make things worse by an ill-conceived amendment that has not been fully deliberated.

But in light of an increasingly active judiciary and the corresponding loss of public faith in its decisions, it is perhaps time to amend the amendment process itself to allow citizens the ability to place a constitutional amendment directly on the ballot for voters to consider and ratify. Such a process can still be deliberative while at the same time ensuring that the people, independent of the legislature, have the power to check the judiciary.

My proposal does exactly that. First, it requires a significantly high threshold—15% of voters in the last gubernatorial election—before the proposed amendment can be placed on the ballot. Only one other state that has ballot initiatives requires a 15% threshold, while the remaining states required only 8% or 10%.

Additionally, it not only requires such a high threshold across the state, but also requires it uniformly throughout the state by dividing the state into sections (each congressional district is divided in ½) in order to ensure wide-spread support for it. Again, only one other state requires such a measure.

Secondly, my proposal requires that the ballot initiative be approved in two of the last three *general* election cycles. No other state with a ballot initiative has this requirement, which guards against an ill-conceived amendment being passed in a fit of temporary passion by the majority. It ensures that two years—the time between general election cycles—passes between votes on the amendment, and prohibits a special election from being called to speed up the process. The process remains deliberative and laborious, but it remains the people's process and not that of party bosses in the legislature.

In addition to groundless fears of progressive liberalism behind the proposal, critics point to California as an example of everything that is wrong with the ballot initiative. Because of the wide-spread use of the ballot initiative in that state, most people commonly associate it with California and, as a result, with liberals. It should first be noted that the vast majority of alleged abuse in California concern proposed statutes or referendums on statutes already passed by the state legislature, while my proposal only concerns constitutional amendments.

Additionally, while California is the most notorious state with ballot initiatives, it is one of only sixteen states where the citizens have such power. The remaining fifteen are: Arkansas, Arizona, Colorado, Florida, Illinois,

Michigan, Mississippi, Missouri, Montana, Nebraska, Ohio, Oklahoma, Oregon, and South Dakota. Because these states are not liberal (in fact, a majority either lean or are reliably Republican0, their ballot initiatives are more moderate and, as a result, get very little notice. One bad example does not prove that the process has no merit.

Finally, no better example of how the ballot initiative can stop judicial activism is the wave of defense of marriage amendments that have swept the nation in the past decade. Thirty states have adopted such amendments, including all but one state that has the option of ballot initiatives. Of those fifteen states with the option of ballot initiatives, nine of their amendments were the result of ballot initiatives rather than legislative initiatives. In several of those states, including California, the amendment never would have seen the light of day if it were dependent upon a vote by the legislature.

There is no better check on judicial activism than the ability of the people to trump an egregiously decided opinion of the court by amending the constitution. The ballot initiative not only allows the people the mechanism to do this without dependence on the legislature, but it allows them to check judicial activism even before the judges strike.

Of the thirty states which have passed marriage amendments, the vast majority did so before their supreme court had an opportunity to strike down their marriage statutes. Unlike a legislature which is purely reactionary, the people can see a looming attack by the judiciary and pass a constitutional amendment before the crises hits.

There is no surer remedy to judicial activism than We The People. As James Madison wrote in Federalist 49: "As the people are the only legitimate fountain of power, and it is from them that the Constitutional Charter under which the several branches of government hold their power is derived, it seems strictly consonant to the republican theory to recur to the same original authority whenever it may be necessary to enlarge, diminish, or new-model the powers of government."

Originally published in *The Iowa Republican* on February 13, 2010.

Nathan W. Tucker

We The People: The Only Cure to Judicial Activism

Nathan W. Tucker